The Night Before Christmas

Written by Clement C. Moore

Illustrated by Tony Tallarico

Kidsbooks®

Visit us at www.kidsbooks.com

Introduction

This unique and entertaining retelling of the seasonal classic *The Night Before Christmas* by Clement Moore, is narrated by two charming elves, **Jingle** and **Belle**. By combining this traditional story with fun Search & Find® activities, we've added a new twist to an old Christmas favorite.

Search & Find® books help sharpen a child's reading, concentration, and cognitive skills. The careful searching for hidden objects enhances young readers' visual dexterity, while the wonderful story and amusing dialogue develop their reading comprehension.

The whole family will have a merry time reading the poem together and searching for all the fun things hidden throughout the book. St. Nick and his eight tiny reindeer are on their way, so get ready to Search & Find® your way through *The Night Before Christmas*!

Belle

Jingle

Search & Find®

Ballo	Ice skates	Telescope
Boa	Kite	Tent
Book	Mask	Tepee
Boomerang	Paintbrush	Train
Crayons (4)	Pencil	Tricycle
Feather	Pizza	Truck
Guitar	Skateboard	U.F.O.
Hammer	Stockings (2)	Windmill
Hockey stick	Straw	Yo-yo

The Night Before Christmas

'Twas the night before Christmas, when all through the house not a creature was stirring, not even a mouse.
The stockings were hung by the chimney with care, in hopes that St. Nicholas soon would be there.

The children were nestled all snug in their beds, while visions of sugarplums danced in their heads.
And Mama in her kerchief and I in my cap, had just settled down for a long winter's nap;

When out on the lawn there arose such a clatter, I sprang from my bed to see what was the matter.
Away to the window I flew like a flash, tore open the shutters and threw up the sash.

The moon on the breast of the new-fallen snow gave the luster of midday to objects below;
When what to my wondering eyes should appear, but a miniature sleigh and eight tiny reindeer,

With a little old driver so lively and quick, I knew in a moment it must be St. Nick!
More rapid than eagles his coursers they came, and he whistled and shouted and called them by name:

"Now, Dasher! Now, Dancer! Now, Prancer and Vixen! On, Comet! On, Cupid! On, Donner and Blitzen!
To the top of the porch, to the top of the wall! Now, dash away! Dash away! Dash away, all!"

As dry leaves that before the wild hurricane fly, when they meet with an obstacle, mount to the sky;
So, up to the housetop the coursers they flew with a sleigh full of toys—and St. Nicholas, too.

And then in a twinkling I heard on the roof the prancing and pawing of each little hoof.
As I drew in my head and was turning around, down the chimney St. Nicholas came with a bound.

He was dressed all in fur from his head to his foot, and his clothes were all tarnished with ashes and soot.
A bundle of toys he had flung on his back, and he looked like a peddler just opening his pack.

His eyes—how they twinkled! his dimples—how merry! His cheeks were like roses, his nose like a cherry!
His droll little mouth was drawn up like a bow, and the beard on his chin was as white as the snow.

The stump of a pipe he held tight in his teeth, and the smoke it encircled his head like a wreath.
He had a broad face and a little round belly that shook when he laughed, like a bowl full of jelly.

He was chubby and plump, a right jolly old elf, and I laughed when I saw him, in spite of myself.
A wink of his eye and a twist of his head soon gave me to know I had nothing to dread.

He spoke not a word, but went straight to his work, and filled all the stockings; then turned with a jerk,
And laying his finger aside of his nose, and giving a nod, up the chimney he rose.

He sprang to his sleigh, to his team gave a whistle, and away they all flew like the down of a thistle.
But I heard him exlaim, ere he drove out of sight, "Happy Christmas to all, and to all a good night!"